# UNIFORMS ILLUSTRATED No 15

UNIFORMS ILLUSTRATED No 15

# French Foreign Legion

## 1940 TO THE PRESENT

### YVES L. CADIOU & TIBOR SZECSKO

a&ap

ARMS AND ARMOUR PRESS

# Introduction

Published in 1986 by Arms & Armour Press Ltd.,
2–6 Hampstead High Street, London NW3 1QQ.

Distributed in the United States by Sterling
Publishing Co. Inc., 2 Park Avenue, New York,
N.Y. 10016.

*British Library Cataloguing in Publication Data:*
Cadiou, Yves
French Foreign Legion 1940 to the present.
– (Uniforms illustrated; 15)
1. France. Armée. Légion étrangère –
Uniforms – History
I. Title    II. Szecsko, Tibor    III. Series
355.3′5    UC485.F8

ISBN 0-85368-806-0

Editing, design and artwork by Roger Chesneau.
Typesetting by Typesetters (Birmingham) Ltd.
Printed and bound in Italy by GEA/GEP in
association with Keats European Ltd., London.

*To the French Foreign Legion and its brave men*

Created in 1831 by King Louis Philippe for the conquest of Algeria, the French Foreign Legion quickly outgrew these rather narrow terms of reference and has, over the years, been involved in all the major campaigns fought by the French Army: Crimea (1854), Italy (1859), Mexico (1863), France (1870 and 1914–18), Dahomey, Sudan, Madagascar, the Tongking region of Indo-China, Morocco, Syria – all these have witnessed the prowess of the Foreign Legion at its best. Since 1940 the Legion has gained a reputation for being an élite corps, its deeds during the Second World War and, later, in South-East Asia and Algeria are well known, and names like Bjervik, Narvik, Bir-Hakeim, Clomar, Caobang, Dien-Bien-Phu, Guelma and Kolwezi will always be associated with it.

The uniform of the legionnaire is basically that of the French infantryman, with its own particular specialities – white-covered *képi*, red and green epaulettes, dark green tie, blue woollen waist-band, seven-flamed grenade and distinctive insignia and badges. The legionnaire is a professional soldier, on duty at all times, and trained for the most dangerous missions. He is enlisted for five years, his average age is 24, and his nationality varies: today, more than one hundred countries around the world can claim to have serving French legionnaires.

The Legion's total strength numbers about 8,500 men. Some 2,800 are stationed on French soil, at Aubagne (1st Regiment, *1er RE*), Orange (1st Cavalry Regiment, *1er REC*), Nimes (2nd Infantry Regiment, *2ème REI*), Calvi, Corsica (2nd Airborne Regiment, *2ème REP*), Castlenaudary (4th Regiment, *4ème RE*) and Avignon (6th Engineer Regiment, *6ème REG*). The rest of the Legion is stationed overseas, in French Guiana (3rd Infantry Regiment, *3ème REI*), Tahiti (5th Regiment, *5ème RE*), Djibouti (13th Half-Brigade, *13ème DBLE*) and on the island of Mayotte in the Indian Ocean (a detachment, *DLEM*). The Legion has its headquarters in Aubagne, under the command of Brigadier-General Roué.

The authors would like to thank the *Service Historique de la Légion Etrangère*, the *Etablissement Cinématographique et Photographique des Armées*, *Képi Blanc* and W.O.1 McCullin of the *1er RE*, without whose assistance this book would have been impossible to prepare.

Yves L. Cadiou and Tibor Szecsko

◀1
1. General Rollet, 'father' of the French Foreign Legion, in 1931. One hundred years after it was founded, the Legion numbered 30,000 men, from fifty countries. Rollet, the Legion's first *Inspecteur-Général*, had by this time served for 36 years, in Madagascar, Algeria and Morocco. During the First World War he had been the commanding officer of the famous *Régiment de Marche de la Légion Etrangère* (Foot Regiment), earning for himself an outstanding reputation as a leader, both in the Legion itself and in the French Army, and as an exceptional administrator. Since his death in 1941 his portrait has hung in every barracks manned by the Legion.

2. The French Foreign Legion (*Légion Etrangère*) was created on 10 March 1831 and originally comprised seven battalions grouped according to nationality; Swiss, Germans, Belgians, Dutch, Italians, Spaniards and Poles were the most numerous, although Frenchmen could enlist provided they declare a foreign nationality. In 1835 this system of segregation was discontinued. The uniform of early legionnaires (shown) consisted of a blue jacket and red trousers, with a shako adorned with a copper emblem on which was stamped a Gallic cock riding a star. The weapon here is the 1822 flintlock Infantry model.

3. The epic Battle of Camerone, 30 April 1863, fought during the Mexican campaign. Under the command of Captain Danjoy, three officers and sixty-two legionnaires died in action against 2,000 Mexicans, of whom 300 perished. This gallant struggle quickly became – and still is – of symbolic significance to the French Foreign Legion: each anniversary is celebrated with great ceremony, and the name 'Camerone' is to be found on its flags.

4. The Legion parades down the Champs Elysées, Paris, 14 July 1939. Here, for the first time, the famous *képi* is part of official dress; previously, the cap cover was olive drab (OD) in colour (although it quickly faded to a whitish hue with frequent washing) and such white *képis* as were worn were done so only at an officer's discretion. The legionnaires are led by Captain Amilakvari, who commanded the Legion at Bir-Hakeim and died at El Alamein in 1942.

◀2

**5.** The 13th Half-Brigade (*13ème DBLE*) on board the SS *Providence* at Brest, February 1940, destination Norway. Clad as alpine troops, with skis, OD berets and sheepskin jackets, the men are soon to experience mountain fighting for the first time.

**6.** The *13ème DBLE* stopped over in Britain on its way to Norway, and was reviewed by the British authorities in Liverpool. Ski-scouts and motorcyclists formed part of the force.

5 ▶

▼ 6

7▲

◄8

7. Following their victories at Bjervik and Narvik, the legionnaires of the *13ème DBLE* pursued their German adversaries towards the Swedish border. Here a support company prepares to fire a light gun; across the men's shoulders are 8mm calibre, 1892-pattern musketoons.

8. A mannequin on display at the Legion's museum in Aubagne, showing the dress of a legionnaire fighting in Norway, May 1940: sheepskin jacket, OD trousers and beret, mountain boots and MAS 1936-pattern 7.5mm bolt-action rifle.

▲9

**9.** Men from the 97th Division Scouting Group (*GRD* 97) pass through a village in the Somme, 1940. The side-cars are equipped with Châtellerault 24/29 7.5mm light machine guns, the motorcyclists themselves with MAS 36 bolt-action rifles. The uniforms comprise leather jackets, heavy linen trousers and special motorcycle helmets.

**10.** After desperate fighting the *GRD 97* tried to cover the retreat of the 7th North African Division as the Germans swept through France in June 1940. This veteran legionnaire, wearing his *Croix de Guerre*, is aiming his Hotchkiss 1914-pattern machine gun. The weapon is fed with rigid 24-round clips of 8mm Lebel calibre.

▼10

**11.** When Syria, then mandated to the French Vichy government, was invaded by British troops in 1941 the 6th Infantry Regiment became involved in the fighting. The photograph shows a Hotchkiss machine gun set up in a pumping station, ready for action. The men's uniforms consist of OD linen summer jackets and trousers, puttees, and the legendary *képi blanc*. Lebel bayonets can be seen hung from the leather waist-belts.
**12.** Men of the 6th Infantry Regiment haul a 75mm gun on to a truck platform. Syria, 1941.

▲13

**13.** After the campaign in Norway the 13th Half-Brigade returned to Britain, where it would form the backbone of the 1st Free French Brigade, a unit that would participate in the 'Desert War' in Libya, 1942. Here one of its legionnaires, dressed in British Army shirt and shorts, raises the green and red standard of the 3rd Battalion on the bayonet scabbard of his rifle.

**14.** The *13ème DBLE* was issued with Bren Gun Carriers for the Libyan campaign, and at Bir-Hakeim the 3rd Battalion formed '*Jock Colonnes*' scouting groups to seek out and engage the enemy.

▼14

15 ▲

**15.** A wounded legionnaire is tended to during the Battle of Bir-Hakeim. The helmets are British Army issue.
**16.** On 10 June 1942, after two weeks of resistance, the garrison at Bir-Hakeim broke the German encirclement: covered by machine-gun fire, the legionnaires counter-attacked and forced their way out. Despite British regulations, the legionnaires elected to wear their *képis blancs* during this famous operation.

16 ▼

**17.** Colonel Miquel reviews the 1st Cavalry Regiment in Tunisia, 11 October 1943. The Legion by this time was largely equipped with US weapons. The regimental band plays in the background.

**18.** The First Cavalry Regiment's trumpeter sounds the departure from Tunisia to France, summer 1944. The pennant is embroidered with the regimental insignia, the figure '1' in the seven-flamed grenade, on a background of green and red (Legion colours) and blue (denoting Cavalry). Note the 'Tunisia' shoulder title.

17▶

▼18

19. British Prime Minister Churchill, accompanied by General de Gaulle, reviews the *Régiment de Marche de la Légion Etrangère (RMLE)* before it departs for Colmar, 13 November 1944. The uniforms and equipment are those of the US Army.

20. Alsace, February 1945: legionnaires free a village occupied by German soldiers.

◀19

20▼

▲21  ▼22

23 ▲

◀24

21. An *RMLE* soldier enters a village in Alsace which has been subjected to heavy artillery fire.
22. An *RMLE* anti-tank gun crew gathers its strength prior to clearing a wood, March 1945.
23. In April 1945 the *13ème DBLE*, which had just taken Strasbourg and Colmar, fought a mountain war in the Alps. Here, preceded by tanks, legionnaires press on towards Italy via an 8,000ft pass.
24. The flag of the *13ème DBLE* flies in Paris for the victory parade, 8 May 1945. The distinctive *képi* with its white cover are the only items of equipment not of US Army issue.

▲25 ▼26

18

27 ▲

◀28

25. With the ending of the Second World War France cast her eyes to the Far East, where survivors of the 5th Infantry Regiment had taken refuge in China following the Japanese invasion. The 2nd Infantry Regiment was the first to return to Indo-China, and from 1946 to 1954 25–30,000 legionnaires contributed to the expeditionary forces, in whose memories the typical coastline scenery of Along's Bay will remain forever engraved.

26. A 2nd Infantry Regiment platoon, back from duties in South Anam, stands to attention for review. The long supply lines from France meant that legionnaires tended to equip themselves with whatever was locally available, but relative uniformity would be established by 1951, thanks to the efforts of General de Lattre.

27. The 13th Half-Brigade perfects its 'Pirogue Patrol' routine to outmanoeuvre the Vietnamese policy of mining the trails, Central Anam, 1947.

28. General Monclar, *Inspecteur* of the Foreign Legion, in Indo-China, 1948. The lady on the right is Susan Travers, a young Englishwoman who enlisted in the Legion in London in 1940 and is the only female ever to have done so. Gaining promotion to the rank of Warrant Officer, and holder of the *Croix de Guerre*, she left the service in 1948 when she married a *13ème DBLE* officer.

▲29  ▼30

31▲

**29.** The survivors of Phu-Tong-Hoa, a small Tonkinese post close to the Chinese border. During the night of 25/26 July 1948 the 104 legionnaires of the *3ème REI* resisted the repeated attacks of three Vietnamese battalions. When relief troops arrived on the scene, 21 men had been killed and forty others wounded.

**30.** *La Rafale* ('The Squall'), a 2nd Infantry Regiment armoured train, in Nha Trang, South Anam. Operated to keep the rail routes clear, the train was hauled by two armoured locomotives and its wagons mounted eight machine guns, a 40mm Bofors gun, a 20mm AA weapon, two mortars and several individual pieces. This photograph shows an 81mm mortar installed on a salvaged Japanese mounting; in the foreground is a US M1 carbine.

**31.** An amphibious operation by the 1st Cavalry Regiment across the Plaine des Joncs (Rush Plain) using 'Crabs' and 'Alligators', 1948.

**32.** The 'Crab' was essentially an M29 cargo carrier adapted for warfare in rice plantations and swamps. It had a crew of four and was generally operated by detachments of six to nine units. The armament consisted of a Browning .30-calibre machine gun, although some 'Crabs' were fitted with heavier weapons such as mortars.

32▼

▲ 33

▼ 34

**33.** A 2nd Squadron, 1st Cavalry Regiment combat unit debusses from an 'Alligator' (a US LVT) in Nam Dinh, Tongking. 'Alligators' operated in detachments of six units and could carry an entire combat platoon fully equipped with heavy machine guns or similar weapons.

**34.** A 2nd Airborne Battalion (*2ème BEP*) paratrooper, having just landed in a rice-field. He wears British style battle-dress and a US helmet and carries a French MAS36/CR39 folding-butt rifle.

**35.** A *2ème BEP* patrol advances through the jungle of North Tongking, 1950. The fourth man is carrying a 1924/29 Châtellerault light machine gun.

**36.** Members of the *1er BEP* move cautiously during the fighting for Colonial Road No 6, November 1951. British camouflaged combat dress is worn, but the weapons are French-made.

▲ 37

▼ 38

**37.** A sudden attack by an invisible enemy on *1er BEP* scouts brings the grenade launcher into action.

**38.** A Vietnamese caught in his own trap. Many legionnaires were injured by this unpleasant device, a short plank bristling with iron spikes and hidden beneath grass.

**39.** The shoulder patch worn by members of the Foreign Legion's 11th Airborne Division (to which the 2nd Airborne Regiment belongs).

**40.** The shoulder patch of the 6th Light Armoured Division (*6ème DLB*).

**41.** The principal regimental insignia of the French Foreign Legion: A. 13th Half-Brigade (*13ème DBLE*); B. 1st Regiment (*1er RE*); C. Command of the Foreign Legion (*COMLE*); D. 4th Regiment (*4ème RE*); E. 5th Regiment (*5ème RE*); F. 2nd Infantry Regiment (*2ème REI*); G. 3rd Infantry Regiment (*3ème REI*); H. 2nd Airborne Regiment (*2ème REP*); I. Detachment of the Foreign Legion, Mayotte (*DLEM*); J. 1st Cavalry Regiment (*1er REC*).

39 ▲

40 ▲  41 ▼

A

B

C

D

E

F

G

H

I

J

LEGIO
PATRIA NOSTRA

3° R E I

D L E M

▲42　▼43

**42.** The 4th Regiment at Castelnaudary trains volunteers, specialists and NCOs (but not officers) for the Foreign Legion. After a four-month training period recruits parade to receive their white *képis* for the first time.

**43.** Members of the 2nd Infantry Regiment with LRAC 89mm rocket launchers at the ready, Corsica, 1982. The battle-dress

uniform is 1963-pattern and the helmet 1968-pattern. Since 1982 the *2ème REI* has been based at Nimes.

**44.** *2ème REI* legionnaires cross a river in Corsica in a VAB light armoured car, 1982.

**45.** Frogmen from the 13th Half-Brigade return from an underwater sortie, Djibouti, 1982.

45▼

▲46 ▼47

46. The Scouting Squadron of the 13th Half-Brigade parades with AMLs and 'jeeps' in Djibouti, 1982.

47. The insignia of the 6th Engineer Regiment (*6ème REG*), comprising a breastplate and helmet, the flaming grenade and the red and green Legion colours. The Roman columns of Baalbeck (Lebanon) are a reminder that this regiment was formed in the Middle East, in 1939. The Latin motto translates to 'Until the Last'.

48. A legionnaire rescues a wounded comrade during the battle for Colonial Road No 6, Indo-China. Not evident is the fact that he is covered from the bushes by his colleagues from the 1st Airborne Battalion.

49. General Salan, Commander-in-Chief of the Foreign Legion, on a visit to the fortified camp at Nasan, December 1952; on his left is Major Brothier, commanding officer of the 1st Airborne Battalion. The green beret with badge was at the time worn in Indo-China only by Legion paratroopers.

50. A 2nd Infantry Regiment platoon during the fighting at Dao Thon, February 1953. A wounded legionnaire is being evacuated.

48 ▲49 ▲  50 ▼

▲51   ▼52

30

53▲

**51.** A 13th Half-Brigade company, led (and commanded) by a lieutenant wearing French battle-dress and a US helmet, on patrol near Dien-Bien-Phu, January 1954.
**52.** Christmas is celebrated at the 'Beatrice' post at Dien-Bien-Phu, held by the 3rd Battalion, the 13th Half-Brigade. This unit retains the 1940-vintage khaki beret worn by French alpine troops.

**53.** A view of the fortifications at Dien-Bien-Phu prior to the withering Vietnamese attacks.
**54.** A Sikorsky S-55 'ambulance' helicopter evacuates wounded legionnaires from Dien-Bien-Phu's medical post. By the end of the battle such evacuation would no longer be possible.

54▼

▲55 ▼56

**55.** The Heavy Mortar Company of the 1st Airborne Regiment in action at Dien-Bien-Phu. The weapon is a 120mm calibre piece.

**56.** Legionnaires of the *1er BEP* just prior to the final assault at Dien-Bien-Phu; on 7 May 1954 the fort would be overrun by the enemy. The garrison comprised some 10,000 men, about half of whom were members of the Foreign Legion. French casualties, killed or wounded, numbered some 8,000, including about 3,000 legionnaires. The Vietminh attacked with 60,000 men, backed up by 150,000 porters and partisans, and suffered casualties numbering about 25,000.

**57.** After Dien-Bien-Phu the Vietminh front-line forces were much reduced, and thousands of legionnaires would continue to fight – but in vain, since the destiny of Indo-China would be decided by other means. This legionnaire awaits orders, but he will soon have to pack up his .30-calibre machine gun and leave for Algeria.

**58.** The year 1955 saw the Foreign Legion stationed in Algeria. By this time it comprised some 20,000 men, with six infantry regiments, two airborne regiments, two cavalry regiments and four Saharan companies. Here the fourteen flags are presented at Sidi-Bel-Abbès, 'home town' of the Legion from 1843 until 1962.

57▲ 58▼

▲59　▼60

**59.** A 3rd Infantry Regiment post on the Moroccan border, a 120mm mortar evident in the foreground. The legionnaires are wearing berets and jungle hats, and the battle-dress is that used in Indo-China. The Algerian *djellaba* (cloak) was a favourite item of clothing during this period.

**60.** A scouting operation in the Djebel Amour, Algeria, February 1957. The group leader (right) is equipped with a US M1 carbine whilst the legionnaire on the left is firing off his MAS 1949/56 semi-automatic rifle. The *képis* have OD covers instead of the usual white covers, and all the men carry regulation rucksacks. The machine gun visible is a French AAT 52.

**61.** Casualty evacuation, Djebel Amour, February 1957.

**62.** Legionnaires from the *3ème REI* scan a desolated region in the Nementchas, Algeria, in 1958. Both men are armed with the French 9mm MAT 49 sub-machine gun. From about this time, the wearing of the green beret and paratrooper-type battle-dress became general practice throughout the Legion.

**61▲   62▼**

▲63　▼64

**63.** Scarcely used in Indo-China, the helicopter assumed great importance in Algeria. The Sikorsky H-34 could carry twelve fully equipped soldiers, here represented by men of the *2ème REI* in the El-Aboid sector. The commander has disembarked first, carrying an MAT 49 sub-machine gun and equipped with three 1937-pattern hand grenades attached to his waist-belt; he is followed by a gunner carrying a Châtellerault FM24/29.

**64.** Legionnaires advance towards the enemy as an H-34 supply helicopter moves overhead.

**65.** Paratroopers train in the skies above Philippeville, Algeria. Nord Noratlas transport aircraft release their human cargo at an altitude of 1,200ft.

**66.** A French Navy Piasecki 'Flying Banana' lands para-troopers near Guelma, Algeria, February 1958.

65▲   66▼

**67.** Men of the 1st Airborne Regiment search for Algerian rebels close to Guelma, April 1958. Skirmishes will be frequent.

**68.** A legionnaire of the *1er RE* is hit by an enemy bullet. Moroccan border, 1958.
**69.** Colonel Jeanpierre, a legendary figure in the history of the Foreign Legion. Commanding officer of the 1st Airborne Regiment in Indo-China and Algeria, he met his death during the Guelma operation in May 1958 when his helicopter was downed by gunfire.

▲70 ▼71

**70.** A display of weapons captured during the fighting around Guelma. In the foreground are a Czech-manufactured recoilless gun and rocket launcher, behind which are arrayed German MG.34 machine guns, Mauser rifles and MP.44 Sturmgewehr assault rifles.

**71.** Light armoured cars (EBR) of the 1st Cavalry Regiment (*1er REC*) operating near Aures, Algeria, in 1958. The crew are wearing the OD linen beret. Note the soldiers' packs attached to the front of the vehicle.

**72.** A Legion doctor attends Algerian youngsters in Aures, September 1958.

**73.** In April 1958, in the Kenchela sector, legionnaires saved the life of a young donkey injured by a bullet and foresaken by its Algerian owner. For this deed the Legion was presented with numerous awards and certificates from various bodies, including the *Société Protectrice des Animaux* and the Royal Society for the Prevention of Cruelty to Animals. The donkey, which was adopted by the legionnaire, seems to be enjoying his unusual journey in this photograph!

72 ▲    73 ▼

**74.** Disgruntled with his lot, a young Algerian rebel surrenders at the *13ème DBLE* post at Aures; he hands over his British-made Lee Enfield rifle to the sentry, who is armed with an MAT 49 sub-machine gun.

**75.** Legionnaires equipped with FAMAS assault rifles and ready for any eventuality.

**76.** Legionnaires disembark from an assault boat and run to their positions. This boat will soon join others to form a pontoon bridge.

▲77   ▼78

A VAB makes
[pro]gress towards the
[batt]le. This vehicle is a
[mo]dern armoured truck
[cap]able of transporting a
[com]plete, fully equipped
[batt]le group.
3rd Infantry
[Re]giment manoeuvres in
[the] Amazon jungle
[ter]rain of French
[Gu]iana: legionnaires
[arm]ed with FAMAS
[rif]les and an 89mm
[LR]AC rocket launcher
[ju]mp to the side of a
[tr]uck to engage an
[im]aginary enemy.
Another view of the
[3è]me REI in the Amazon
[ju]ngle, with an AAT52
[lig]ht machine gun ready
[for] firing. The AAT52
[ha]s a calibre of 7.5mm
[bu]t can be converted
[in]to a heavy machine
[gu]n by changing its
[ba]rrel. Cyclic rate of fire
[is] 700 rounds per minute
[in] light configuration
[an]d 900 rounds in heavy
[co]ndition. The crew
[he]re comprises three
[m]en wearing camou-
[fla]ged battle-dress.
In French Guiana
[th]e best way to get
[ar]ound is by river, the
[3è]me REI here making
[th]e most of the circum-
[st]ances. River patrols
[fo]rm an important part
[of] the scouting mission
[cl]ose to the Brazilian
[bo]rder, and every
[le]gionnaire knows how
[to] man a canoe.

79 ▲    80 ▼

▲81　▼82

**81.** A mortar section (*3ème REI*) on manoeuvres on the island of Guadeloupe.

**82.** Part of the 5th Regiment's duty involves work on the Mururoa Atoll in the Pacific Ocean – the French nuclear test centre. This giant mechanical shovel holds no secrets for its legionnaire driver.

**83.** The 2nd Saharan Company (*2ème CSPL*) on patrol around Laghouat, 1959: the captain commanding the company receives the report of the cameleer scout and decides to trail the enemy. He is wearing the French 1958-pattern camouflaged battle-dress and a *cheche* (a long scarf which can be wound into a sort of turban) around his neck. His rank is displayed on his epaulettes.

**84.** The 2nd Saharan Company on parade at Laghouat on 30 April 1958 – 'Camerone Day'. The vehicles visible are Dodge 6×6 weapons carriers and AM.8 light armoured cars. The Company CO is in the foreground, and to his right is the horsetail-decorated standard held by an NCO wearing a black *képi* and guarded by two legionnaires armed with MAS 36 rifles, bayonets fixed. All the men are wearing the Saharan parade uniform, comprising white jacket, wide *seroual* trousers of blue linen with an Agadir cross embroidered on each side, a double-folded blue and white cape (burnous), red trimmings and Saharan sandals.

83▲   84▼

▲85 ▼86

**85.** In 1959 4th Infantry Regiment companies spread across the Eastern Erg, some even reaching El Oued. In this photograph a 6×6 weapons carrier is armed with a 1924/29-pattern light machine gun and packs are hung on the vehicle's sides.
**86.** Algerian rebels and weapons captured by the *4ème REI* following operations around Bir-el-Ater, 1960.
**87.** After the cease-fire in Algeria in 1962 the *2ème REI* was sent south to defend military posts in the desert. Legionnaires were issued with special dress for wear in this sector – OD *djellaba*, Saharan *seroual* trousers (with 32 creases), sandals, and *képi* with neck cover.
**88.** In 1962 the 1st Regiment took up quarters at Aubagne in the south of France, which would become the new 'home' for the Legion. The same year the Legion was invited to parade down the Champs Elysées on 14 July.

**89.** The principal band of the French Foreign Legion, in Aubagne. The musicians are wearing the winter parade uniform comprising white *képi*, woollen jacket (with traditional red and green epaulettes) and trousers and white gauntlets and gaiters. The side drums are fitted with red and green drapes and are hung low to cope with the legionnaires' slow march.

**90.** Training was quickly re-established in Corsica in 1962. Here a legionnaire scales an obstacle during a combat proficiency course.

**91.** How to kill a tank: a legionnaire, hidden in a foxhole, positions a mine in the path of an oncoming vehicle.

**92.** Firing a 60mm mortar on the Agriates desert ranges in Corsica.

93. The French Foreign Legion has always had a reputation for high-quality engineering and construction. In 1963 special training courses were held at Nimes for the 5th Regiment, who would later fly out to Tahiti to make ready the Pacific nuclear test centre.

94. Stationed at Calvi in Corsica, the 2nd Airborne Regiment headquarters has become a sort of 'laboratory' for testing and experimenting in the techniques of modern warfare. As soon as he enlists in the *2ème REP* a legionnaire is taught to jump; the regiment supervises over 25,000 such jumps annually.

95. Specialist teams are trained for day and night operations from both submarines and surface ships.

96. Frogmen from the *2ème REP* prepare themselves before being dropped into the sea.

▲ 93    ▼ 94

95▲  96▼

55

**104**

**104.** Members of the *3ème REI* clear trees in initial preparations for
the building of the Ariane launching site in French Guiana.
**105.** French Guiana provides excellent terrain for perfecting
techniques in jungle combat. In this photograph a *3ème REI*
legionnaire readies his AAT52 light machine gun during a training
exercise in the Kourou region. The seven-flamed grenade insignia is
prominent on his beret.
**106.** Companies of the *3ème REI* on parade at Kourou. These men,
from the most decorated regiment in the French Army, are wearing
the triple braided *fourragère* and are equipped with the French

1949/56-pattern semi-automatic rifle. The captain and an NCO are
wearing paratroopers' wings, despite the fact that this is an infantry
regiment.
**107.** Since 1969 the French Foreign Legion has been called three
times to Chad at the request of the government there. Here, in
1970, two patrols, one from the *2ème REP* and the other from the
*1er RE*, exchange information. The *1er RE* officer, right, wears the
'Satin 300' battle-dress while his opposite number wears the 1957-
pattern camouflaged battle-dress.

▼**105**

▲97

**97.** Each unit of the *2ème REP* specializes in a particular aspect of warfare. This is a sabotage team.
**98.** In addition to his basic qualifications a *2ème REP* legionnaire might become a deadly sniper, using the famous French FR-F1

rifle. Note the wing-and-dagger badge, denoting Airborne troops, on this man's green beret.
**99.** Members of the 2nd Infantry Regiment (*2ème REI*) haul a 120mm mortar at their Nîmes headquarters.

▲100

**100.** Legionnaires undergo training in the use of the Model FI 89mm anti-tank weapon.

**101.** Following its arrival at Orange in 1967 the 1st Cavalry Regiment was issued with Panhard light armoured cars (AML) equipped with a 90mm gun. The commander can be distinguished by his black *képi*.

**102.** Legionnaires in action with a Milan anti-tank missile launcher in Djibouti.

**103.** Men from the *3ème REI* assist the local populace: a regimental doctor here checks up on a youngster in French Guiana.

▼101

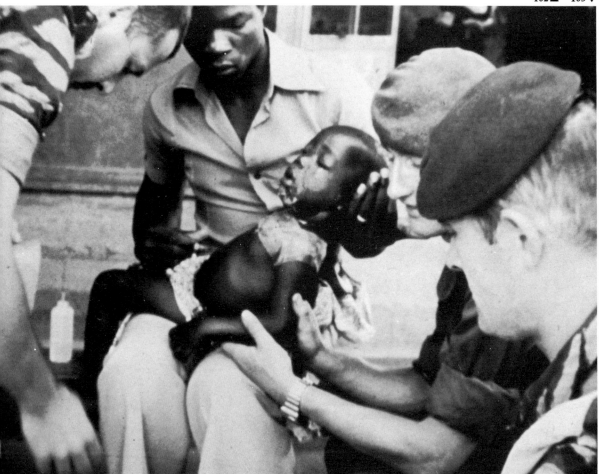

▲108    ▼109

**108.** On 3 February 1976, in Djibouti, terrorists captured a school bus aboard which were thirty children. Legionnaires from the 1st Cavalry Regiment and the 2nd Airborne Regiment stormed the bus at Loyada, near the Somali border, and rescued all the young hostages.

**109.** In May 1978 the *2ème REP* found itself operating in Zaïre, nearly 4,000 miles from its home base in Corsica. Here, at 7.00am on the 19th, Legion paratroopers are seen preparing for their drop over Kolwezi. Some difficulty is being experienced with the US parachutes, which are being used for the first time and have to be adapted to the French harnesses.

**110.** Some of the 650 legionnaires dropping over Kolwezi, 3.30pm, 19 May.

**111.** The paratroopers are welcomed with short bursts of machine-gun fire but, happily, suffer no casualties.

111▼

▲112

▼113

**112.** From 22 May Kolwezi and the surrounding countryside were cleared of rebels.
**113.** Mission fulfilled: legionnaires of the *2ème REP* have saved 2,500 European lives.
**114.** The aftermath of the operation around Kolwezi: more than 250 rebels have been killed and over 1,000 weapons seized. Losses to the *2ème REP* are five men killed and 25 wounded.
**115.** President Mobutu of Zaïre and Colonel Erulin review the legionnaires of the *2ème REP*. For the occasion the troops are clad in camouflaged battle-dress and wear the green beret.

114▲   115▼

▲116    ▼117

**116.** Troops from the *2ème REP* prepare to embark on an Air Zaïre wide-bodied jet, 7 June 1978. The destination is their base at Calvi in Corsica.

**117.** Beirut, Lebanon, 21 August 1982: the 2nd Airborne Regiment of the Foreign Legion, part of the French Rapid Intervention Force, embarks on a peace-keeping role, preceding the Multi-National Peace-Keeping forces and permitting the fighters of the PLO an honourable retreat.

**118.** Colonel Coullon, sent to Beirut by the French Minister of Defence, discusses the situation with a Syrian Army officer. On his return to France a few days after this photograph was taken, Coullon was promoted to head the Legion, in which he had spent the majority of his military career.

**119.** After the departure from Beirut of the PLO, the security of the population became the responsibility of the *2ème REP* until 13 September 1982. In this photograph a sentry, wearing the 'Satin 300' battle-dress and armed with a FAMAS assault rifle, keeps watch from his sandbagged position near the harbour.

118▲ 119▼

◀120           121▲           122▲   123▼

**120.** The Legion in 1985. The legionnaire in the background is equipped with an FR-F1 sniper's rifle fitted with a Model 53*bis* telescopic sight and folding bipod. The officer listens to his TRPP.11 walkie-talkie, and has an MAC 50 automatic pistol in its canvas holster at his waist. All three men are wearing the 'Satin 300' battle-dress and green beret.

**121.** A legionnaire of the 2nd Airborne Regiment in winter parade uniform, comprising woollen jacket and trousers (1946-pattern), white *képi*, fringed epaulettes, green tie and blue woollen waist-band. The regimental insignia and paratroopers' wings are worn on the right breast, and the Airborne dagger hangs from his canvas waist-band. The red *fourragère* of the *Legion d'Honneur*, worn *en bataille* with the parade uniform, hangs beneath the left arm.

**122.** A *2ème REB* bugler in winter parade uniform. The pennant is of green velvet with red stripes and, in the centre, the embroidered regimental badge.

**123.** A *pionnier* (pioneer) from the 1st Regiment in summer parade uniform, 1970. All *pionniers* are bearded (according to tradition) and are responsible for all barracks maintenance work. They thus comprise masons, electricians, locksmiths, painters, carpenters and so on. Each Foreign Legion regiment has one pioneer section, who always lead parades, clad in yellow leather aprons and carrying their axes on their right shoulders.

▲124 ▼125

**124.** The Foreign Legion on parade in the Champs Elysées, 1983. This regiment is disposed in marching order – the *pionniers*, the band, the colonel, the flag and its guard and finally the companies. The soldier nearest to the camera is WO1 Janet, *Chef des Pionniers*, who jumped over Kolwezi.

**125.** The principal band of the Foreign Legion at Aubagne, 'Camerone Day', 1980. The band comprises approximately 100 musicians. The famous *Chapeau Chinois* (literally, 'Chinese hat') is a tradition that can be traced back to the old 'Army of Africa': it was originally an Arabian instrument equipped with small bells and shaken during marches. The horsetails are, according to Arabian legend, those of the animals of a defeated enemy.

**126.** Men of the 2nd Airborne Regiment on manoeuvres in Corsica. The weapon is an AAT52 light machine gun of 7.5mm (or NATO 7.62mm) calibre and the battle-dress is 1963-pattern. Note the Airborne badge on the green beret.

**127.** Personnel from the 2nd Infantry Regiment undergo training with a Model F1 LRAC 89mm anti-tank launcher, 1980. The men are wearing 1956-pattern camouflaged battle-dress and green berets.

▲128　▼129

**128.** Men from the 1st Cavalry Regiment train in their Panhard AML near Orange, France, 1981. The 90mm gun will quickly find its target.
**129.** Legionnaire in the jungle: a member of the Foreign Legion detachment on the island of Mayotte in the Indian Ocean pauses during a patrol. The sub-machine gun is an MAT 49.